Traynor

by Iain Gray

D1385721

LangSyne
PUBLISHING
WRITING *to* REMEMBER

Lang Syne

PUBLISHING

WRITING *to* REMEMBER

Office 5, Vineyard Business Centre,
Pathhead, Midlothian EH37 5XP
Tel: 01875 321 203 Fax: 01875 321 233
E-mail: info@lang-syne.co.uk
www.langsyneshop.co.uk

Design by Dorothy Meikle
Printed by Hay Nisbet Press, Glasgow
© Lang Syne Publishers Ltd 2009

ISBN 978-1-85217-339-5

Traynor

MOTTO:
By law and right.

CREST:
A lion.

NAME variations include:
Mac Thréinfhir (*Gaelic*)
Trainor
Tranor
Treanor
Trenor

Chapter one:
Origins of Irish surnames

**According to an old saying, there are two types of Irish –
those who actually are Irish and those who wish they were.**

This sentiment is only one example of the allure that the
high romance and drama of the proud nation's history holds
for thousands of people scattered across the world today.

It's a sad fact, however, that the vast majority of Irish
surnames are found far beyond Irish shores, rather than on
the Emerald Isle itself.

The population stood at around eight million souls in
1841, but today it stands at fewer than six million.

This is mainly a tragic consequence of the potato
famine, also known as the Great Hunger, which devastated
Ireland between 1845 and 1849.

The Irish peasantry had become almost wholly reliant
for basic sustenance on the potato, first introduced from the
Americas in the seventeenth century.

When the crop was hit by a blight, at least 800,000
people starved to death while an estimated two million
others were forced to seek a new life far from their native
shores – particularly in America, Canada, and Australia.

The effects of the potato blight continued until about
1851, by which time a firm pattern of emigration had
become established.

Ireland's loss, however, was to the gain of the countries in which the immigrants settled, contributing enormously, as their descendants do today, to the well being of the nations in which their forefathers settled.

But those who were forced through dire circumstance to establish a new life in foreign parts never forgot their roots, or the proud heritage and traditions of the land that gave them birth.

Nor do their descendants.

It is a heritage that is inextricably bound up in the colourful variety of Irish names themselves – and the origin and history of these names forms an integral part of the vibrant drama that is the nation's history, one of both glorious fortune and tragic misfortune.

This history is well documented, and one of the most important and fascinating of the earliest sources are *The Annals of the Four Masters*, compiled between 1632 and 1636 by four friars at the Franciscan Monastery in County Donegal.

Compiled from earlier sources, and purporting to go back to the Biblical Deluge, much of the material takes in the mythological origins and history of Ireland and the Irish.

This includes tales of successive waves of invaders and settlers such as the Fomorians, the Partholonians, the Nemedians, the Fir Bolgs, the Tuatha De Danann, and the Laigain.

Of particular interest are the *Milesian Genealogies*,

because the majority of Irish clans today claim a descent from either Heremon, Ir, or Heber – three of the sons of Milesius, a king of what is now modern day Spain.

These sons invaded Ireland in the second millennium B.C, apparently in fulfilment of a mysterious prophecy received by their father.

This Milesian lineage is said to have ruled Ireland for nearly 3,000 years, until the island came under the sway of England's King Henry II in 1171 following what is known as the Cambro-Norman invasion.

This is an important date not only in Irish history in general, but for the effect the invasion subsequently had for Irish surnames.

'Cambro' comes from the Welsh, and 'Cambro-Norman' describes those Welsh knights of Norman origin who invaded Ireland.

But they were invaders who stayed, inter-marrying with the native Irish population and founding their own proud dynasties that bore Cambro-Norman names such as Archer, Barbour, Brannagh, Fitzgerald, Fitzgibbon, Fleming, Joyce, Plunkett, and Walsh – to name only a few.

These 'Cambro-Norman' surnames that still flourish throughout the world today form one of the three main categories in which Irish names can be placed – those of Gaelic-Irish, Cambro-Norman, and Anglo-Irish.

Previous to the Cambro-Norman invasion of the twelfth century, and throughout the earlier invasions and settlement of those wild bands of sea rovers known as the Vikings in the eighth and ninth centuries, the population of the island was relatively small, and it was normal for a person to be identified through the use of only a forename.

But as population gradually increased and there were many more people with the same forename, surnames were adopted to distinguish one person, or one community, from another.

Individuals identified themselves with their own particular tribe, or 'tuath', and this tribe – that also became known as a clann, or clan – took its name from some distinguished ancestor who had founded the clan.

The Gaelic-Irish form of the name Kelly, for example, is Ó Ceallaigh, or O'Kelly, indicating descent from an original 'Ceallaigh', with the 'O' denoting 'grandson of.' The name was later anglicised to Kelly.

The prefix 'Mac' or 'Mc', meanwhile, as with the clans of the Scottish Highlands, denotes 'son of.'

Although the Irish clans had much in common with their Scottish counterparts, one important difference lies in what are known as 'septs', or branches, of the clan.

Septs of Scottish clans were groups who often bore an entirely different name from the clan name but were under the clan's protection.

In Ireland, septs were groups that shared the same name and who could be found scattered throughout the four provinces of Ulster, Leinster, Munster, and Connacht.

The 'golden age' of the Gaelic-Irish clans, infused as their veins were with the blood of Celts, pre-dates the Viking invasions of the eighth and ninth centuries and the Norman invasion of the twelfth century, and the sacred heart of the country was the Hill of Tara, near the River Boyne, in County Meath.

Known in Gaelic as 'Teamhar na Rí', or Hill of Kings, it was the royal seat of the 'Ard Rí Éireann', or High King of Ireland, to whom the petty kings, or chieftains, from the island's provinces were ultimately subordinate.

It was on the Hill of Tara, beside a stone pillar known as the Irish 'Lia Fáil', or Stone of Destiny, that the High Kings were inaugurated and, according to legend, this stone would emit a piercing screech that could be heard all over Ireland when touched by the hand of the rightful king.

The Hill of Tara is today one of the island's main tourist attractions.

Opposition to English rule over Ireland, established in the wake of the Cambro-Norman invasion, broke out frequently and the harsh solution adopted by the powerful forces of the Crown was to forcibly evict the native Irish from their lands.

These lands were then granted to Protestant colonists, or 'planters', from Britain.

Many of these colonists, ironically, came from Scotland and were the descendants of the original 'Scotti', or 'Scots', who gave their name to Scotland after migrating there in the fifth century A.D., from the north of Ireland.

Colonisation entailed harsh penal laws being imposed on the majority of the native Irish population, stripping them practically of all of their rights.

The Crown's main bastion in Ireland was Dublin and its environs, known as the Pale, and it was the dispossessed peasantry who lived outside this Pale, desperately striving to eke out a meagre living.

It was this that gave rise to the modern-day expression of someone or something being 'beyond the pale'.

Attempts were made to stamp out all aspects of the ancient Gaelic-Irish culture, to the extent that even to bear a Gaelic-Irish name was to invite discrimination.

This is why many Gaelic-Irish names were anglicised with, for example, and noted above, Ó Ceallaigh, or O'Kelly, being anglicised to Kelly.

Succeeding centuries have seen strong revivals of Gaelic-Irish consciousness, however, and this has led to many families reverting back to the original form of their name, while the language itself is frequently found on the fluent tongues of an estimated 90,000 to 145,000 of the island's population.

Ireland's turbulent history of religious and political strife is one that lasted well into the twentieth century, a landmark century that saw the partition of the island into the twenty-six counties of the independent Republic of

Ireland, or Eire, and the six counties of Northern Ireland, or Ulster.

Dublin, originally founded by Vikings, is now a vibrant and truly cosmopolitan city while the proud city of Belfast is one of the jewels in the crown of Ulster.

It was Saint Patrick who first brought the light of Christianity to Ireland in the fifth century A.D.

Interpretations of this Christian message have varied over the centuries, often leading to bitter sectarian conflict – but the many intricately sculpted Celtic Crosses found all over the island are symbolic of a unity that crosses the sectarian divide.

It is an image that fuses the 'old gods' of the Celts with Christianity.

All the signs from the early years of this new millennium indicate that sectarian strife may soon become a thing of the past – with the Irish and their many kinsfolk across the world, be they Protestant or Catholic, finding common purpose in the rich tapestry of their shared heritage.

Chapter two:

Sons of the strongman

A name that is deeply rooted in the soil of the ancient Irish province of Ulster, the Gaelic-Irish form of Traynor – 'MacThréinfhir' – means 'son of the strongman', or 'son of the champion.'

It was these 'sons of the strongman' who for centuries held sway in the barony of Truagh, in Co. Monaghan – this at a time when Monaghan was one of the nine counties that then made up Ulster.

It was not until the foundation of the Irish Free State and the partition of the island in 1922 that the previous Ulster counties of Monaghan, Donegal and Cavan were recognised as part of the Free State – leaving Ulster with the remaining counties of Antrim, Armagh, Tyrone, Fermanagh, Londonderry and Down.

But not all bearers of the Traynor name to be found on the Emerald Isle today are of original Ulster stock.

In later centuries bearers of the name, in this case derived from the Anglo-Saxon 'trayne', indicating 'trapper', came to Ireland from Durham and York, in England.

Adding further confusion to the Traynor pedigree is that while many Scots of the name of Armstrong also settled in Ireland, some Armstrongs are actually of original Traynor stock.

This arose because in some cases the Gaelic-Irish 'Mac Thréinfhir' indicating, as noted, 'son of the strongman', was mistranslated and anglicised in some cases to 'Armstrong.'

In common with the Armstrongs of original Scottish stock, however, the Gaelic-Irish Traynors are of ancient lineage.

Their pedigree is truly regal, descended as they are from Ireland's earliest monarchs.

In the case of the Traynors, this is from Heremon who, along with Heber, Ir and Amergin, was a son of Milesius, a king of what is now modern day Spain, and who had planned to invade the island in fulfilment of a mysterious Druidic prophecy.

Milesius died before he could embark on the invasion, but his sons successfully undertook the daunting task in his stead in about 1699 B.C.

Legend holds that their invasion fleet was scattered in a storm and Ir killed when his ship was driven onto the island of Scellig-Mhicheal, off the coast of modern day Co. Kerry.

Only Heremon, Heber and Amergin survived, although Ir left issue.

Heremon and Heber became the first of the Milesian monarchs of Ireland, but Heremon later killed Heber in a quarrel said to have been caused by their wives, while Amergin was slain by Heremon in an argument over territory.

Along with the Traynors, other clans that trace a descent

from Heremon include those of Cassidy, Donnelly, Higgins, Kelly, McKenna, McManus, Callaghan and O'Connor.

Many distinguished Irish kings were of the noble line of Heremon.

They include Irial Fiada, one of his sons, and the 10th monarch of Ireland. Recognised as very learned and with the gift of second sight, it was Irial, who died in 1670 B.C., who was responsible for clearing much of the island of its dense forests.

Also of the Heremon line of kings was Tigernmas, the 13th monarch of Ireland.

Said to have worshipped a mysterious idol known as 'Crom Cruach', it was Tigernmas who introduced the wearing of colours as a means of distinguishing rank.

A soldier would wear three colours, while a king or queen would wear six – and some authorities assert this may be the origins of the plaid, or tartan, worn centuries later by those originally native Irish who had settled in the Highlands and Islands of Scotland.

The 66th monarch of the line of Heremon, Ugaine Mór, appears to have been particularly enterprising.

This king, who died in 593 B.C., is reputed to have landed with a force of Celtic warriors in Africa, while he later married a daughter of the king of the Gauls.

But arguably the most notable of the Heremonian line of Irish monarchs was Cormac Mac Art.

Recognised as the wisest of the original Milesian line,

he ruled his kingdom from the Great Hall of Tara, aided by a loyal retinue of 1,150 people.

He died in 266 A.D. – several years after abandoning the Druidic faith in favour of Christianity.

The Traynors forged a particularly close bond with their fellow Heremonian descendants the, McKennas.

An area known as Emyvale in the north of Co. Monaghan was for centuries the homeland of the McKennas.

An explanation of how they came to settle there in about the eighth century A.D. can be found on the clan's coat of arms – that features the figure of a hunter on horseback, his two hounds, a stag, and two crescent moons.

The two crescent moons are symbolic of the two days and nights that a McKenna chieftain from the area of Kells, in present day Co. Meath, had spent in pursuit of the stag.

He and his faithful hounds finally ran it to bay at what is now Liskenna, in Emyvale.

It was here that he plunged his dagger, or dirk, into the beast's heart – and this may well provide an explanation for the McKenna motto of 'sons of the dirk'.

Exhausted after his long and arduous expedition, the McKenna hunter gratefully accepted the hospitality of a local chieftain known as Treanor, or Traynor – who was so impressed with the young man's hunting skills and charm that he offered him his daughter's hand in marriage.

After several weeks of enjoying the hospitality of Treanor and the bridal charms of his daughter, the McKenna chieftain received word that his own kingdom had been usurped in his absence by rival kinsfolk.

Rather than travelling back to his former kingdom with his young bride, he decided to settle in Emyvale – becoming the founder of a dynasty of McKennas that would rule for centuries, in close alliance with the Traynors, as the Lords of Truagh, in what was a territory of roughly eighty square miles.

The clan's headquarters were established at Tully, near Liskenna, and it was here that they built an imposing series of ring forts atop a hill while a fortification was also erected in the middle of a nearby lake.

To the south of the Traynor and McKenna territory lay the homeland of the McMahons, while to the north lay the territories of the powerful O'Neills.

While not fighting among themselves for control of the lordship of Truagh, the Traynors and McKennas were also frequently at war with the O'Neills and the McMahons – much in the same manner that their Celtic counterparts in the Highlands and Islands of Scotland were also often engaged in destructive warfare with one another.

It was this disunity that was to ultimately have disastrous consequences for the native Irish clans such as the Traynors, as invaders from foreign shores exploited it to their advantage.

This was illustrated to dramatic and tragic effect in the late twelfth century.

Chapter three:

Invasion and rebellion

By 1156 the most powerful of Ireland's kings was Muirchertach MacLochlainn, King of the Traynor neighbours, the O'Neills.

He was opposed by the equally powerful Rory O'Connor, King of the province of Connacht, but he increased his power and influence by allying himself with Dermot MacMurrough, King of Leinster.

MacLochlainn and MacMurrough were aware that the main key to the kingdom of Ireland was the thriving trading port of Dublin that had been established by invading Vikings, or Ostmen, in 852 A.D.

Their combined forces took Dublin, but, when MacLochlainn died, the Dubliners rose up in revolt and overthrew the unpopular MacMurrough.

A triumphant Rory O'Connor entered Dublin and was later inaugurated as Ard Rí, but MacMurrough refused to accept defeat.

He appealed for help from England's Henry II in unseating O'Connor, an act that was to radically affect the future course of Ireland's fortunes.

The English monarch agreed to help MacMurrough, but distanced himself from direct action by delegating his Norman subjects in Wales with the task.

These ambitious and battle-hardened barons and knights had first settled in Wales following the Norman Conquest of England in 1066 and, with an eye on rich booty, plunder and lands, were only too eager to obey their sovereign's wishes and furnish MacMurrough with aid.

He crossed the Irish Sea to Bristol, where he rallied powerful barons such as Robert Fitzstephen and Maurice Fitzgerald to his cause, along with Gilbert de Clare, Earl of Pembroke.

The mighty Norman war machine soon moved into action, and so fierce and disciplined was their onslaught on the forces of O'Connor and his allies that by 1171 they had re-captured Dublin, in the name of MacMurrough, and other strategically important territories.

Henry II now began to take cold feet over the venture, realising that he may have created a rival in the form of a separate Norman kingdom in Ireland.

Accordingly, he landed on the island, near Waterford, at the head of a large army with the aim of curbing the power of his Cambro-Norman barons.

But protracted war between the King and his barons was averted when they submitted to the royal will, promising homage and allegiance in return for holding the territories they had conquered in the King's name.

Henry also received the submission and homage of many of the Irish chieftains, tired as they were with internecine warfare and also perhaps realising that as long as they were rivals and not united they were no match for the powerful forces the English Crown could muster.

English dominion over Ireland was ratified through the Treaty of Windsor of 1175, under the terms of which Rory O'Connor, for example, was allowed to rule territory unoccupied by the Normans in the role of a vassal of the king.

Two years earlier, Pope Alexander III had given Papal sanction to Henry's dominance over Ireland, on condition that he uphold the rights of the Holy Roman Catholic Church and that chieftains adhere rigorously to the oaths of fealty they had sworn to the English king.

While many Irish clans were reluctantly forced to seek an accommodation with the Crown, others took a defiant stance of resistance – not least clans such as the Traynors, McKennas and the O'Neills, who now found themselves belatedly united in the face of a common foe.

One indication of the harsh conditions under which they suffered, as the Crown's grip on the island tightened like a noose around their necks, can be found in a desperate plea sent to Pope John XII by Roderick O'Carroll of Ely, the Traynor ally Donald O'Neill of Ulster, and a number of other Irish chieftains in 1318.

They stated: 'As it very constantly happens, whenever an Englishman, by perfidy or craft, kills an Irishman, however noble, or however innocent, be he clergy or layman, there is no penalty or correction enforced against the person who may be guilty of such wicked murder.

'But rather the more eminent the person killed and the higher rank which he holds among his own people, so much more is the murderer honoured and rewarded by the English, and not merely by the people at large, but also by the religious and bishops of the English race.'

This written plea had no effect on English policy and, rather than trusting in the power of the pen, native Irish clans resorted to the power of the sword.

This had truly devastating consequences for the island, resulting in the eventual destruction of the ancient and noble Gaelic order of clans such as the Traynors.

Discontent had grown on the island over the policy known as 'plantation', or settlement of loyal Protestants on lands held by the native Irish. This policy had started during the reign from 1491 to 1547 of Henry VIIII, whose Reformation effectively outlawed the established Roman Catholic faith throughout his dominions – and continued throughout the subsequent reigns of Elizabeth I, James I (James VI of Scotland), Charles I, and in the aftermath of the Cromwellian invasion of the island in 1649.

The island was blighted by bloody rebellions in reaction to plantation – rebellions that ultimately proved abortive.

Rebellion in a most spectacular form occurred in the form of the 1916 Easter Rising in Dublin – a Rising in which the politician and revolutionary Oscar Traynor played a role. Born in 1886 in Dublin, it was as a member of the Irish Volunteers that Traynor was involved in the Rising.

As the bitter struggle for Irish independence from British rule had intensified, the Irish Citizen Army (I.C.A.), that had been founded by James Connolly, joined forces with the Irish Republican Brotherhood (I.R.B.) to mount the Easter Rising of 1916, known in Irish as *Éiri Amach na Cásca*, following a proclamation of independence signed by Connolly and six others.

With Connolly as Commandant of the Dublin Brigade, the aim was to wrest independence from Britain by force of arms and, accordingly, on April 24, Easter Monday, the combined Republican forces of the I.C.A. and the I.R.B. seized strategic locations throughout Dublin, including the General Post Office.

Other Risings were timed to take place simultaneously throughout the counties of Galway, Wexford and Louth.

With a force of less than 5,000 Republicans matched against no less than 16,000 well armed and trained troops and 1,000 armed police, the Rising was doomed to failure – coming to a bloody and exhausted conclusion on April 30 after its leaders were forced into reluctant surrender.

More than 1,200 Republicans, troops, police and civilians had been killed, but further deaths followed as the sixteen leaders of the Rising, including James Connolly, were executed by the British Crown in Dublin's Kilmainham Jail.

Oscar Traynor was captured and interned for a time in Wales and, five years later during the Irish War of

Independence as Brigadier of the Dublin Brigade of the Irish Republican Army (I.R.A.), he led an attack on the Custom House.

During the bitter and bloody Irish Civil War that erupted in June of 1922, Traynor was part of the Republican force that occupied what is now Dublin's O'Connell Street, in a bid to aid fellow Republicans who had occupied the Four Courts.

After a week of street fighting between the Republicans and soldiers of the Irish Free State, Traynor and his companions managed to flee Dublin and wage a campaign of guerrilla warfare in Co. Wicklow before being captured.

Imprisoned for the duration of the Civil War, by March of 1925 Traynor had discarded the gun in favour of the ballot box and was elected to the Irish Parliament, Dáil Éireann, as the Sinn Féin member for Dublin North.

By 1932, as a member of the Fianna Fáil political party, he was again elected to parliament and later served in a number of top Cabinet posts – including Minister for Sports and Telegraphs, Minister for Defence and, before his retirement from politics in 1961, as Minister of Justice.

Traynor had been a gifted footballer as a young man, touring Europe as one of the star players of the Belfast Celtic club.

It was in recognition of his passion for football that in 1948 he was appointed President of the Football Association of Ireland – a post he held until his death in 1963.

Chapter four:

On the world stage

Bearers of the Traynor name, in all its variety of spellings, have achieved fame and distinction in a wide range of pursuits and callings.

One bearer of the name in particular gained fame in a truly miraculous manner when, after journeying to the Roman Catholic pilgrim centre at Lourdes, in France, he was cured of severe wounds he had received during the terrible carnage of the First World War.

This was **Jack Traynor**, who was born in Liverpool in 1878 and who joined the Naval Brigade of the British Royal Marines at the beginning of the war.

Hit in the head by shrapnel during the abortive Antwerp raid of October 1914, he remained unconscious for four weeks.

Despite this he was later able to fight in Egypt, where he received a bullet wound in the leg, while he was wounded in the head, chest and arm while fighting later in the Gallipoli campaign.

This left him with his right arm and his legs partially paralysed, while in April of 1920 a silver plate was inserted in his skull after an operation to remove shrapnel.

His medical condition was so bad that it was recommended he be transferred from his family home in

Liverpool to a hospital for incurables, but Traynor, in 1923, insisted on accompanying fellow Catholics to Lourdes.

It was on June 25, while immersed in the waters of one of the healing baths, that his legs suddenly began to show movement. Shortly after this, a procession led by the Archbishop of Rheims, who was carrying the Blessed Sacrament, passed by the baths and blessed the bathers.

To Traynor's astonishment, he was able to move his right arm in order to bless himself. Later that evening, he was able to rise from his bed and walk to the Grotto to pray.

News of his apparent miraculous cure spread rapidly, and, when he arrived back home, hundreds of people were waiting to greet him at the railway station.

Fully recovered from his war wounds, he managed to run a successful coal delivery business until his death at the age of 65, while he was also a regular visitor to Lourdes in the capacity as a voluntary stretcher-bearer for pilgrims unable to walk.

Also on the field of battle, **William Traynor** was an English recipient of the Victoria Cross, the highest award for gallantry for British and Commonwealth forces.

Born in 1870 in Hull, Yorkshire, he had been a sergeant in the 2nd Battalion, The West Yorkshire Regiment, during the Boer War.

During an enemy night attack in February of 1901 at Bothwell Camp, South Africa, he ran out of a trench, under extremely heavy fire, to help a wounded comrade.

He was shot and wounded while doing so but, with the aid of a fellow soldier, he was able to carry the wounded man back to shelter.

Despite his own wounds, Traynor remained in command of his section, encouraging his men until the enemy attack failed.

In contemporary times, **Bernard E. Trainor** is the retired U.S. Marine Corps lieutenant general who was born in 1928 in New York City.

A recipient of the Distinguished Service Medal, two Legions of Merit and the Bronze Star, he is a former Chief of Operations for the U.S. Marine Corps and member of the U.S. Joint Chiefs of Staff.

He is also the author of a number of books on military matters, including the 1995 *The Generals' War: The Inside Story of the Conflict in the Gulf.*

Bearers of the name have also excelled, and continue to excel, in the highly competitive world of sport – particularly that of European football.

Born in 1963 in Glasgow, **Mark Treanor** is the former professional Scottish footballer who began his career in 1979 with Clydebank.

Other teams that the right-back played for until his retirement in 1994 included St. Johnstone and Stranraer.

Born in Dundalk in 1933, **Tommy Traynor** was the Irish footballer who was a leading player with English team Southampton between 1952 and 1966.

The player, who died in 2006, also won eight Republic of Ireland national team caps between 1954 and 1964.

Tommy Traynor was also the name of a talented Scottish footballer who was born in 1943 in Bonnybridge, Stirlingshire.

The winger, who played for clubs that included Hearts, Dundee United, Morton and Falkirk, later immigrated to Melbourne, Australia, where he died in 1993.

In contemporary European football, **Robert Traynor**, born in 1983 in Burnham, Buckinghamshire, is the player who has played for teams that include Brentford and Kingstonian.

In the world of football punditry, **Jim Traynor** is the Scottish sports journalist with the Daily Record newspaper who also presents the popular BBC Scotland football-based phone-in programme *Your Call*.

In the equally fast-paced game of ice hockey, **Paul Traynor** is the former Winnipeg Jets player who was born in 1977 in Thunder Bay, Ontario, and who, at the time of writing, plays for the Iserlohn Roosters of the German Hockey League.

In the world of baseball, Harold Traynor was the American professional third baseman better known as **Pie Traynor**.

Born in 1898 in Framingham, Massachusetts, he spent his entire career from 1920 to 1937 with the Pittsburgh Pirates.

Recognised as having been one of the greatest National League third basemen, Traynor, who was elected to the Baseball Hall of Fame in 1948, died in 1972.

In contemporary baseball, **Matthew Treanor**, born in 1976 in Garden Grove, California is, at the time of writing, a catcher for the Florida Marlins.

He is married to the American professional beach volleyball star **Misty May-Treanor**, who was born in 1977 in Santa Monica, California.

From sport to the stage, **Mary Ellen Trainor** is the American actress born in Chicago in 1950 and who is best known for her role as Dr. Stephanie Woods in the movie *Lethal Weapon* and its three sequels.

Other films she has appeared in include *The Goonies*, *Romancing the Stone* and *Forrest Gump*, while from 1999 to 2002 she was one of the stars of the popular *Roswell* television series.

Born in San Diego in 1977, **Jerry Trainor** is the American film and television actor whose film roles include *Donnie Darko* and *Bring It On Again* and whose television roles include *Law and Order*, *Angel* and *Malcolm in the Middle*.

In the world of music, **Jay Traynor**, born in 1943 in Albany, New York, is the former lead vocalist of the top-selling band Jay and the Americans, whose first hit was *She Cried*.

Leaving the band to pursue an equally successful solo

career, he now tours with the band Jay Siegel and The Tokens.

Born in 1954 in Charlottetown, Prince Edward Island, **Frank Trainor** is the popular Canadian singer and songwriter whose releases include the 2005 *Grace and Gravity* and the 2008 *Pockets Full of Paradise*.

In the legal world, **Roger Traynor**, born in 1900 in Park City, Utah, to Irish immigrant parents, is recognised as having been not only the greatest judge in the history of the Californian justiciary, but also one of the greatest judges in the history of the United States.

He served from 1964 to 1970 as the 23rd Chief Justice of the Supreme Court of California, and was responsible for a number of landmark legal rulings, including the creation of true strict liability in product liability cases. The judge, who died in 1983, was described in his obituary in the *New York Times* as 'one of the greatest judicial talents never to have sat on the United States Supreme Court.'

In contemporary times, **William Treanor**, born in 1957, is the American attorney and noted legal scholar who served from 1998 to 2002 as deputy assistant attorney general in the U.S. Justice Department's Office of Legal Counsel.

In the ecclesiastical sphere, **Bishop Noel Treanor**, born in 1950 in Silverstream, Co. Monaghan, is the Irish prelate of the Roman Catholic Church who was appointed 32nd Bishop of the Diocese of Down and Connor, in Northern Ireland, in June of 2008.

Taking to the skies and the outer limits of space, **Dr. James H. Trainor**, born in 1935 in Lancaster, New Hampshire, was the distinguished American scientist who served with the National Aeronautics and Space Administration (NASA) from 1964 to 1994.

An associate director and chief scientist of NASA's Goddard Space Flight Center in Greenbelt, Maryland, Dr. Trainor, who died in 2003, was a recipient of the agency's medal for Distinguished Service and a Meritorious Rank Presidential Award from President Ronald Reagan.

Key dates in Ireland's history from the first settlers to the formation of the Irish Republic:

circa 7000 B.C. Arrival and settlement of Stone Age people.

circa 3000 B.C. Arrival of settlers of New Stone Age period.

circa 600 B.C. First arrival of the Celts.

200 A.D. Establishment of Hill of Tara, Co. Meath, as seat of the High Kings.

circa 432 A.D. Christian mission of St. Patrick.

800-920 A.D. Invasion and subsequent settlement of Vikings.

1002 A.D. Brian Boru recognised as High King.

1014 Brian Boru killed at battle of Clontarf.

1169-1170 Cambro-Norman invasion of the island.

1171 Henry II claims Ireland for the English Crown.

1366 Statutes of Kilkenny ban marriage between native Irish and English.

1529-1536 England's Henry VIII embarks on religious Reformation.

1536 Earl of Kildare rebels against the Crown.

1541 Henry VIII declared King of Ireland.

1558 Accession to English throne of Elizabeth I.

1565 Battle of Affane.

1569-1573 First Desmond Rebellion.

1579-1583 Second Desmond Rebellion.

1594-1603 Nine Years War.

1606 Plantation' of Scottish and English settlers.

1607	Flight of the Earls.
1632-1636	Annals of the Four Masters compiled.
1641	Rebellion over policy of plantation and other grievances.
1649	Beginning of Cromwellian conquest.
1688	Flight into exile in France of Catholic Stuart monarch James II as Protestant Prince William of Orange invited to take throne of England along with his wife, Mary.
1689	William and Mary enthroned as joint monarchs; siege of Derry.
1690	Jacobite forces of James defeated by William at battle of the Boyne (July) and Dublin taken.
1691	Athlone taken by William; Jacobite defeats follow at Aughrim, Galway, and Limerick; conflict ends with Treaty of Limerick (October) and Irish officers allowed to leave for France.
1695	Penal laws introduced to restrict rights of Catholics; banishment of Catholic clergy.
1704	Laws introduced constricting rights of Catholics in landholding and public office.
1728	Franchise removed from Catholics.
1791	Foundation of United Irishmen republican movement.
1796	French invasion force lands in Bantry Bay.
1798	Defeat of Rising in Wexford and death of United Irishmen leaders Wolfe Tone and Lord Edward Fitzgerald.

1800	Act of Union between England and Ireland.
1803	Dublin Rising under Robert Emmet.
1829	Catholics allowed to sit in Parliament.
1845-1849	The Great Hunger: thousands starve to death as potato crop fails and thousands more emigrate.
1856	Phoenix Society founded.
1858	Irish Republican Brotherhood established.
1873	Foundation of Home Rule League.
1893	Foundation of Gaelic League.
1904	Foundation of Irish Reform Association.
1913	Dublin strikes and lockout.
1916	Easter Rising in Dublin and proclamation of an Irish Republic.
1917	Irish Parliament formed after Sinn Fein election victory.
1919-1921	War between Irish Republican Army and British Army.
1922	Irish Free State founded, while six northern counties remain part of United Kingdom as Northern Ireland, or Ulster; civil war up until 1923 between rival republican groups.
1949	Foundation of Irish Republic after all remaining constitutional links with Britain are severed.